Five Plays to Read, Discuss and Write About

PAUL GROVES
NIGEL GRIMSHAW

HODDER AND STOUGHTON
LONDON SYDNEY AUCKLAND TORONTO

British Library Cataloguing in Publication Data
Groves, Paul
   Reactions: five plays to read, discuss
   and write about.
   1. Secondary schools. Activities: Drama—
   For schools
   I. Title   II. Crimshaw, Nigel
   792'.07'12

   ISBN 0-340-49340-2

First published in Great Britain 1988

© 1988 Paul Groves and Nigel Grimshaw

All rights reserved. No part of this publication may be reproduced or transmitted in any form or by any means, electronically or mechanically, including photocopying, recording or any information storage or retrieval system, without either the prior permission in writing from the publisher or a licence permitting restricted copying. In the United Kingdom such licences are issued by the Copyright Licensing Agency, 33–34 Alfred Place, London WC1E 7DP

Typeset in Garamond by Wearside Tradespools, Fulwell, Sunderland
Printed and bound in Great Britain for Hodder and Stoughton Educational, a division of Hodder and Stoughton Ltd, Mill Road, Dunton Green, Sevenoaks, Kent by Page Bros (Norwich) Ltd

CONTENTS

	Page
Teacher's Introduction	1
Student's Introduction	3
Who are the Beasts?	5
Situation Vacant	15
The Concert	28
Boat Trip	40
Let's have a Party	60

Teacher's Introduction

These plays are relatively complete in themselves and have been written so that they are easy to read and no character has long speeches to cope with. They are, however, intended to be a basis for discussion and extension and can provide useful practice in oral and written work leading to GCSE for both less-able and mixed-ability classes.

At certain stages of the action in each play, the students are invited to discuss how the situation at this juncture might be developed and then asked to improvise in groups a continuation of that scene. This can be done simply, with the group considering what further events might follow depending on decisions already taken in the play or, with a more sophisticated group, their continuation of the action could arise from their assessment of the characters in the play and their ideas on how each one might react to given events.

Each version of these group improvisations might be discussed afterwards and the most effective in terms of dramatic effect and relevance could be scripted for inclusion in the final version of the play.

For the more skilful class 'dramatists' we have included suggestions indicating how the plot might be expanded and where characters external to the play may be brought in and these could also provide material for discussion and improvisation. We have indicated how we think this process might be done in the 'Student's Introduction'.

We have ordered the plays so that the early ones have simpler, more prescriptive suggestions for expanding the action while the suggestions in later plays are more open-ended.

At the end of the book we have included suggestions for written work, dividing these into categories which we think are easier and those which are more difficult. We have thought about such matters as casting, production, dramatic techniques and staging and tried to phrase assignments on these suitable both for the less and the more imaginative student. Question One is intended to be the easier question.

Student's Introduction

Each of these plays is fairly complete in itself but suggestions are given at the end of each play for making it longer. So you can take part in making a final version of every play. You could go about it like this.

Read Through. Select the people to play the characters and read through the play. You will obviously want to know what the play is about and what happens in it but, if you can, try to get some idea of what the characters in the play are like. Read it, too, as if you were speaking the lines and not simply reading the words to yourself. You will have to think about the emphasis you give to what you say and how the character you are playing feels about it.

Discuss Developments. At the end of each play you are given a lead as to how scenes can be continued or how the plot can be developed. Read these and, taking each one in turn, discuss in a group what you think might happen and how characters might react.

Improvise the Scene. After each discussion play out, in character, the line of events you have discussed. You will have to make up your own words for the characters you are playing. If you do this in groups you will present to the class various versions of what might happen.

Discuss the Improvised Scenes. Some of these scenes may contain a twist that other groups have not considered. In some scenes, characters may not behave as one might expect; they may behave 'out of character' and may be unconvincing or surprising. Discuss each of the scenes and then decide which is most effective or which scene was most liked by people in the class.

Script the Scene. The people in the group whose scene has been chosen could then write out their scene and, if possible, make enough copies of it for each of the characters in the scene to have one. It might be that people outside the group, during the discussion, have suggested other things for the characters to say or extra dialogue. This could be put into the script.

Perform the Play. If you wish, you could then either perform or tape the whole play bringing in the scenes you have created and written.

WHO ARE THE BEASTS?

―― *Characters in the play* ――
Lucy	Master of the Hunt
Tania	Huntswoman
John all age 17	**Mrs Ford**, Lucy's mother
Morry	**Mr Ford**, Lucy's father

―― *Characters for Scene One* ――

Lucy   John
Tania   Morry

Scene One   In **Lucy**'s room in her house. They are discussing sabotaging a fox hunt.

Tania Got the map?
Lucy Here. It's one of the new scale ones so it's right up to date.
Tania Where's Hellington?
Lucy There.
John How far's that from here?
Lucy About fifteen miles.
Morry That's a long way.
Lucy Nothing on a bike.
Morry A motor-bike perhaps, but not a push-bike.
Lucy You are feeble.
Tania I don't think he really wants to do it. No bottle.
Morry No, I'm keen.
John We'll have to be there early.
Lucy Yes, the hunt meets at eight. I want us to have finished doing the aniseed trails by seven. Now look, I've pencilled out where we lay them, to put the hounds off the scent. Look. This one leads round in a circle back

John	to the village. And this one leads to the motorway which they can't cross. I'll make photocopies of this so we all have one.
Lucy	Have you got the aniseed, Morry?
Morry	Not yet. But I can get it.
Tania	You won't let us down, will you?
Morry	Of course I won't let you down.
Lucy	Let's get down to the details. I reckon we need to be there at five so we'll have to leave here before the sun comes up. We'll need lights on the bikes.
John	What will your parents say, girls?
Lucy	They won't know. I'll say something about going to college early and not wanting any breakfast.
Tania	Me too.
Lucy	Let's decide on the route to get there then I'll show you the placards I've made.

⟨1⟩──────────────────────────────────────

```
┌─────────── Characters for Scene Two ───────────┐
│                                                │
│         Lucy       Tania                       │
│         John       Master of the Hunt          │
│         Morry      Huntswoman                  │
│                                                │
└────────────────────────────────────────────────┘
```

Scene Two At the Hunt's meet on Hellington village green.

Lucy and friends	Save the fox! Save the fox! (*They parade round*)
Huntswoman	Little nuisances! Shall we teach them a lesson, Master?
Master	No, I'll speak to them. I suppose you think this is all very clever?
Tania	Not clever, just humane.

Master You think we're not humane?
Lucy You're neither humane or human. Who could kill a creature in cold blood like you do?
Master I suppose you don't enjoy a good T-bone steak.
Lucy I'm a vegan.
Master You do want to see foxes in the countryside? Well, the hunt stops people just gassing and shooting them to extinction.
John Tell that to the fox.
Master You townspeople don't understand the countryside and its ways. You think of foxes as furry little pets. Foxes and hunting have gone together for hundreds of years. It's a time-honoured way of life.
Morry Ways that need to be brought up-to-date. Would you like to be pursued by hounds and torn to pieces as you drop in exhaustion?
Master You obviously don't know how clever the fox is.
Morry What's that got to do with it? You can't be clever when you're dead.
Master If we gave up fox hunting it would put many people in the countryside out of work and see the extinction of the fox in a very few years. We preserve foxes!
John That's a red herring. You bastard!
Huntswoman It's no good reasoning with them, Master.
Master Obviously not.
Huntswoman They're little interfering know-alls!
Master Come on. (*Blows horn*)

Characters for Scene Three

Lucy   John
Tania   Morry

Scene Three *The four friends are standing excitedly in a field near Hellington.*

John What a success!
Lucy Another fox saved!
Tania Did you just see those hounds go round in circles? I could have died laughing.
Lucy That fat bloke fell off his horse in annoyance. Hope he broke his leg.
Morry I think we had better go before they come after us.
John No chance. They don't know whether they are coming or going.
Tania Shall we save the placards or dump them?
Lucy Save them for next time.

(They go behind a wall for their bikes)

Morry I say, look at my bike wheel!
John And mine. Someone's kicked the spokes in.
Lucy They're all damaged. That's the kind of people we're dealing with.
Morry It'll be a long walk back pushing these.
John Leave them. I'll get my brother to come in his van. We'll hide them in the hedge.
Lucy Come on. We'll have to walk home. But it was worth it.

(They walk for some time. Feeling weary, they stop near a large, ugly building)

John What's that place? Looks like a prison camp . . .

Morry It says Brampton Research Station.
Lucy Yes, and we all know what they research.
Morry What?
Lucy They experiment on animals. For cosmetics most likely.
Tania No, they're testing cures for illnesses. I read about the work somewhere.
Lucy Cures! Can you imagine the torture those animals endure being injected and shaved and such like?
Morry I suppose it has to be done.
Lucy Look, are you one of us? Thousands of animals are tortured in laboratories up and down the country. If they want to experiment to cure human illnesses why don't they do it on humans?
Morry I suppose you're right, really.
John The gateman is looking at us.
Lucy Come on.

3

Characters for Scene Four

The same as in Scene Three

Scene Four The four friends are holding a meeting in **Lucy**'s room to decide whether to protest against the Brampton Research Station.

Morry Do you think we should?
John I'm with her.
Morry She's just mad about what happened to the bikes and wants to get her own back on people who ill-treat animals.
John Come on! It's more than that. This could be a bigger success than the hunt sabotage.
Morry That wasn't against the law. This is.

John We won't be caught so it doesn't matter.
Morry Yes, but it's breaking and entering Government property.
John You needn't. You can be the look-out.
Morry I don't know.
John Chicken.
Morry I'm not chicken.

(**Lucy** *and* **Tania** *come in*)

Lucy I've discovered the gateman is not there at night.
Tania Yes, and better still, you can crawl under the fence round the back.
Morry There must be an alarm of some sort.
Lucy John's thought of that.
John My Dad installs them. So I know how to put them out of action! I'll see if I can find out where the alarm box is.
Morry There could be more sophisticated devices.
Lucy We've got to take some chances for the sake of the animals.
Morry I just don't think we should.
Lucy You'll have the deaths of animals on your conscience.
Tania We need you as a look-out.
Morry I don't know. I don't know.
Lucy If you chicken out, Morry, that's an end to our relationship. I couldn't go out with a boy who wouldn't do all he could for animals.
Morry Oh but I do . . . Oh, all right, but be careful in there.

> **Characters for Scene Five**
> **Lucy   Tania   John**

Scene Five Inside the Brampton Research Station. It is night. The three friends use torches to look around them.

Lucy A piece of cake.
John Fancy finding that window open. Someone was careless.
Lucy Shine the torches over there.
Tania Rabbits. Let's let them out.
John If only we could give them good homes.
Lucy At least they'll stand some chance running free.
Tania Look. Dogs. I always thought so. Open the cages. I'd love that one.
Lucy You can't keep it Tania. If we let it go someone might give it a good home. Oh, look at that monkey!
John You can't let that go. It could die out there.
Lucy It'll die in here.
Tania No, Lucy, be sensible. It's cold outside.
Lucy I'll just give it a cuddle. (*Opens cage*) Ouch!
Tania What's up?
Lucy It's bitten me.
John Badly?
Lucy It's bleeding a lot.
John Let's see. That's a deep bite. Have we any bandages?
Lucy I didn't think of that.
Tania You should have.
Lucy I thought of everything else, damn it! Ow!
John Look at that notice.
Lucy Give me a hanky. I'm really bleeding.

John Look at that notice. IF BITTEN REPORT IMMEDIATELY TO MEDICAL OFFICER.
      Lucy, you must go to a doctor.
Lucy I can't do that. Don't be so stupid.
Tania You must, Lucy.
Lucy No, I'll be all right.

5

Characters for Scene Six

Lucy
Mrs Ford
Mr Ford

Scene Six At the local hospital. Lucy is in bed with a bandaged arm. Her parents are with her.

Mrs Ford How are you feeling?
Lucy   Hot.
Mrs Ford You will be for a bit the nurse said.
Mr Ford   What a good thing Morry phoned us when he did. You could have died, pet.
Lucy   I've been daft, haven't I. Are the police going to prosecute me?
Mr Ford   Don't you worry about that now. I'll see to it. You just concentrate on getting better.
Lucy   I hope they prosecute. It will let the public know what dreadful diseases they give animals.
Mrs Ford There. There. Try to rest.
Lucy   Can I see Morry?
Mrs Ford Later. It's only family at the moment.
Lucy   Cor, I must be ill!
Mr Ford   But you're getting better. Promise you'll never do anything like this again.
Mrs Ford Not now, Jack.

12

Lucy It's all right, Mum, I won't. But you do know how I feel about animals.
Mrs Ford Yes, dear, we know.

Work on the play

① Continue the Scene

They discuss the route by looking at the map. They look at Lucy's placards. They discuss contacting TV and the local press.

Develop the Plot

Lucy's parents, Mr and Mrs Ford, discuss what Lucy is up to in her room. Mr Ford thinks they are planning a super disco. Mrs Ford is not sure. She says Lucy has been very secretive lately. She nags Mr Ford into having a talk to her.

② Continue the Scene

Tania, John, Lucy and Morry continue to shout to all the members of the hunt as they go off.

Develop the Plot

Mr and Mrs Ford discover their daughter is not there and has left a note that is untrue. They begin to ring round to find out where she is as she is not at college. You could begin when the college phone to ask where she is.

③ Continue the Scene

They continue on their way for a while, but Tania decides to go back to the station for another look. She asks Lucy to come with her. The boys are not keen, but they all return to scout around the back of the research station. The boys are worried the gateman will send for the police.

Develop the Plot

Lucy gets home at 3 pm and is questioned by her parents who say they were worried sick and nearly went to the police. Lucy stalls them by saying that she and Tania have been out to the countryside to gather information for a biology project and they had a crash on their bicycles.

④ Continue the Scene

The boys go. Tania discusses with Lucy whether she would really give up Morry. We see how fanatical Lucy is.

Develop the Plot

They meet and go into detail about what equipment they need for the break-in. Lucy has planned it carefully for midnight the next Wednesday. Morry is still very unsure about the project.

OR

You could do the actual break-in.

⑤ Continue the Scene

The others try to persuade Lucy to go to a doctor. She says that the truth about their activities could come out if she does. They argue. John takes her out to Morry but she still refuses.

Develop the Plot

There could be a TV report of the incident with the reporter appealing urgently for the intruders to get in touch with their doctors. It could take place in the Ford's home with Mr and Mrs Ford having no idea that the report concerns their daughter. How could you do this dramatically?

SITUATION VACANT

Characters in the play

Miss Starr, receptionist
Leslie Thomas, age 17
Deborah Houseman, age 16
Sharon Connors, age 17
Blair Errol, age 16
Samantha Eagle, age 18
Geoffrey Wilson, age 16

Characters for Scene One

Miss Starr
Leslie Thomas
Deborah Houseman

Scene One   The outer office of Mr Universe's suite at the Universal Trading Company Limited. **Miss Starr** sits at a computer and there are a number of empty chairs.

Leslie   (*Comes in hesitantly*) Excuse me. Is this the office for the interview? The doorman's instructions were not very clear.

Miss Starr   He's very old. You must forgive him.

Leslie   Oh, I thought he looked young.

Miss Starr   (*Avoiding argument*) Name please?

Leslie   Leslie Thomas.

Miss Starr   (*Refers to computer*) Yes, you have come to the right place.

Leslie   I'm not late am I? My watch seems to have stopped. (*He looks round but there is no clock*)

Miss Starr   No, you are not late, Leslie. Nobody has ever been late. Just take a seat.

(**Deborah** *comes in. She looks anxious*)

Deborah Is this room 77, please? It doesn't say on the door.
Miss Starr I'm sorry we have to keep changing the number. The new number is obviously not in place yet. Can I help you?
Deborah I've come about the job.
Miss Starr Name please?
Deborah Deborah Houseman.
Miss Starr Just a minute. (*Works computer*) Yes, you have come to the right place. Please sit down.

(*She exits.* **Leslie** *and* **Deborah** *avoid each other's glance. They are silent for a while. Then* **Leslie** *plucks up courage*)

Leslie What job have you come for?
Deborah Is there more than one then?
Leslie I don't know. I have come for the filing clerk and computer trainee job.
Deborah Oh. So have I.
Leslie Oh.
Deborah (*After a pause*) A very tall building this. The lift seemed to go on for ages.
Leslie Lift? I got lost coming up the stairs.
Deborah I got lost too. I went down a lot of corridors looking for this number. It wasn't on the door.
Leslie I thought I saw it on the door.
Deborah Oh. (*In disbelief*)
Leslie Well, I saw it somewhere. Perhaps it was on a wall in the corridor.

> ┌─────── *Characters for Scene Two* ───────┐
> Miss Starr   Deborah Houseman
> Leslie Thomas   Blair Errol

Scene Two   The office. **Miss Starr** at the computer.
(**Blair** enters)

Deborah   Have you come for the job?
Blair   Is this the place?
Leslie   For the filing clerk job?
Blair   That's it.

(**Leslie** looks at **Deborah** and pretends to cut his throat)

Deborah   We're here for it too.
Blair   Oh.

(**Miss Starr** returns)

Blair   I'm Blair Errol.
Miss Starr   Just let me check. (Works computer) I have a Blair Thomas but no Errol.
Blair   I used to be called Thomas, till my mother remarried.
Miss Starr   Ah, our files cannot be up-to-date. Most unusual.
Blair   I put Errol on the form.
Miss Starr   That's all right, Mr Errol. I can change it.

(She exits)

Blair   (Waiting for her to go) That's odd. How do they have my old name? I remember putting Errol on the form.
Deborah   You could be mistaken. I do funny things when filling in forms, because I don't like doing it I suppose.
Leslie   Must be these computers. I hope I'll be able to manage one. (Pause) That's if they pick me, of course.

Deborah	I don't stand a chance. I don't know why they sent for me. I've no GCSEs.
Blair	I've got six.
Leslie	You must be the favourite then. I've got two. One is in English. No, you must be the favourite.
Deborah	There could be others yet.

```
┌─────────────Characters for Scene Three─────────────┐
│  Miss Starr              Blair Errol               │
│  Leslie Thomas           Samantha Eagle            │
│  Deborah Houseman        Geoffrey Wilson           │
└────────────────────────────────────────────────────┘
```

Scene Three The office. **Miss Starr** *has left the room.*
(**Samantha** *enters*)

Samantha	You others waiting for an interview for the filing clerk job?
Leslie	You see, there are others.
Deborah	Yeh.
Samantha	I've found the right place at last. I think I got off the escalator wrongly.
Deborah	But there was a lift, not an escalator.
Samantha	I didn't see a lift. I came up the escalator.
Deborah	You must have come in another door.
Blair	Well, I came up . . .

(**Miss Starr** *returns*)

Miss Starr	Name please.
Samantha	Samantha Eagle.
Miss Starr	(*Works Computer*) Yes, Miss Eagle, take a seat. Mr Universe will see you all very soon.
Samantha	Is that his real name?
Miss Starr	What would you expect him to be called?

(**Miss Starr** *goes*)

Samantha I don't think it's his real name.
Leslie Well, it's called the Universal Trading Company.
Samantha No-one would be called Mr Universe. I should think it's some gimmick. I hope it's a respectable firm. I've been to some shady interviews in my time. My Mum says be careful.
Deborah I've never seen such a posh building.
Blair Yes, those fountains.
Deborah I didn't see any fountains. I was thinking of the carpets. It was like walking on air.
Leslie Yeh, like walking on the clouds.
Samantha Could just be the front for some shady business. The Mafia could be behind it.
Deborah Oh, you don't think that do you?
Samantha My Mum says be careful.

(**Geoffrey** *enters. He is extremely nervous*)

Geoffrey Am I late? Has it started? I missed the bus.
Leslie No.
Geoffrey Then I got lost in that long tunnel.
Deborah What tunnel?
Geoffrey You know that one after the blue door. The one that goes on for miles and miles. Or so it seems.
Blair What blue door?

> Characters for Scene Four
>
> **The same** as in Scene Three

Scene Four *The office.* **Miss Starr** *at the computer.*

Miss Starr Ah, you must be Geoffrey. Geoffrey Wilson.
Geoffrey How did you know?
Miss Starr You're the last on my list.
Samantha So there're five of us.
Geoffrey Sorry I'm late. I missed the bus. Still I suppose I will be interviewed last. My name beginning with 'w'. I don't like to be early. I get all nervous.
Miss Starr You are not late Geoffrey. Nobody is ever late. I'll see if Mr Universe is ready.

(**Miss Starr** *goes. They sit in silence for some seconds*)

Blair Like waiting for the guillotine, isn't it?
Samantha Doesn't worry me. I've been to so many interviews. Look at him. (*Referring to* **Geoffrey**) He's biting his fingers off.
Geoffrey I can't help it.
Leslie What do you think the advert meant by long holidays?
Deborah I didn't know it said that.
Leslie It was in the Gazette.
Blair I saw it in an agency window.
Samantha I saw it on Ceefax.
Deborah I was rung up by the Job Centre. I think it was them.
Geoffrey I got a letter.
Leslie How odd we all know about it in different ways.
Samantha It was a funny application form too. On blue paper – very thin paper.

Blair Yes, I found some of the questions odd. I mean that one about charity . . .

(**Miss Starr** *returns*)

Miss Starr Mr Universe will see you first, Geoffrey.
Geoffrey But I'm a 'w'.
Miss Starr Mr Universe will see you first.

Characters for Scene Five

The same as in Scenes Three and Four

Scene Five Two hours later. The office is getting darker. **Miss Starr** *is not at the computer.*

Samantha (*Returning*) What an interview! He seemed to know what I was going to say before I said it. There's something weird about this job.
Leslie Isn't he old?
Deborah And that beard. Reminded me of Father Christmas.
Blair He didn't seem that old to me.
Geoffrey More like middle-aged.
Blair I'd put him younger. And that funny suit.
Samantha Yeh, just what was it made of?
Blair Well, he didn't have much to say . . . and he didn't give much away . . . I tried to find out about the job.
Samantha Not talk much? He asked me question after question.
Geoffrey He didn't have a beard did he?
Deborah Of course he had a beard.
Geoffrey I must have been so nervous I didn't notice.
Samantha Well, who's the lucky one? I know it isn't me.

Leslie	(*Getting up*) I can't sit still. (*He wanders round*) I say this window's odd. You can see out of it, but you can't see anything.
Blair	(*Getting up*) Let me see. It must be because we're so high up.
Leslie	Well, you should look down on other buildings. But there's nothing.
Deborah	It could be special glass. Sort of reflective. Something to do with keeping in the heat.
Leslie	I expect that's it.
Miss Starr	(*Returning*) Mr Universe would like to see you, Geoffrey.
Geoffrey	Me?
Miss Starr	Yes, you. Don't sound so surprised.

◇ 5 ───────────────

┌─────── Characters for Scene Six ───────┐
Samantha	Deborah
Leslie	Blair
└──┘

Scene Six   The office. **Miss Starr** *is not at the computer.*

Samantha	That's it then. He's got the job. We can go home.
Leslie	We'd better wait. You never know. Miss Starr didn't say go. What's the time? My watch has stopped.
Deborah	Ten past two. No, I think mine has stopped as well.
Samantha	I seem to have lost mine. Perhaps I didn't put it on.
Blair	I haven't got one.
Leslie	It can't be ten past two. We've been here for hours.
Deborah	Yes, it has stopped.
Leslie	There's no clock. Can you see one?

Deborah Funny office.
Samantha Yes, I've been right all along. Anyway it's a waste of time waiting. I've been to so many interviews. I know the form. I'm going. (*She gets up*) I say.
Deborah What?
Samantha The door I came in by. Where is it?
Deborah There's the door.
Samantha I didn't come in by that. I came through a double door.
Blair That's right, so did I.
Samantha I must go out by the same door. I'll get lost in a building like this.
Leslie I was too nervous to notice what door I came in by. I expect you were the same.
Samantha I wasn't nervous. I know the door I came in by.
Deborah A door can't change. Try that door.
Samantha (*Goes to door and opens it*) It's dark. There are no lights. I'm not going down there. The way I came was brightly lit.
Leslie I'd call it more subtle lighting the way I came.
Deborah We must wait for Miss Starr to come back. Funny name. It's here on her desk.
Samantha I'm not waiting. (*She goes to the door of Mr Universe's room and knocks*)
Leslie You'll catch it, knocking on there.

(*They wait for some time. There is no reply.* **Samantha** *knocks again, harder*)

Samantha I'll have to go in. I'm frightened. There's something very odd about all this. (*She tries the door*) It's locked!

23

Characters for Scene Seven

Samantha	Blair
Leslie	Miss Starr
Deborah	Sharon Connors

Scene Seven *The office. It has now become very dark.* **Miss Starr** *is not at the computer.*

Leslie Mr Universe could still be interviewing Geoffrey.

Samantha No we're trapped in here. Can't you see!

Blair How can we be trapped when there's a door out? Do calm down.

Samantha You open it and see. (*She cries*)

Deborah It's all right, love.

Blair (*Opens door*) Yes, it is dark. Just a minute I'll let my eyes get accustomed to it. I can see a long passageway and some stairs going down, I think. Come on.

Leslie I still think we should wait. It's rude just to go. There could be other jobs here.

Samantha I'm not working here. Let's shout.

Leslie No, that's silly.

Deborah Let's just go.

Samantha I'm dead scared. (*Shouts*) Help! Help!

(*Her voice echoes back. Then there is silence.* **Blair** *also shouts. His voice echoes*)

Samantha Let's go. (*To* **Blair**) Will you lead the way?

Blair Sure.

Samantha Let me hang on to you.

Blair (*To* **Leslie**) Coming?

Leslie Oh, all right.

(*They all go out of the door*)

Their Voices	It's warm. It's getting darker. I can't see. It's cold!
	(*They die away.* **Miss Starr** *returns. She shows no surprise at the empty office. She works on the computer. It whirrs away for some time.* **Sharon** *comes in*)
Sharon	Have I got the right room?
Miss Starr	Name please.
Sharon	Sharon Conners.
Miss Starr	(*Refers to computer*) Yes, Miss Connors, take a seat. There are others to come. Mr Universe will see you in a moment.
	(*The lights slowly fade*)

Work on the play

After you have read this play discuss what you think it is about before you do any work on it. Why is it mysterious? What are you not told? Where might the real setting be?

 Continue the Scene

Leslie and Deborah discuss whether the Universal Trading Company Ltd might want a boy or girl for the job.

Develop the Plot

Miss Starr returns and asks them certain personal questions. They are not the sort of questions you would expect at an interview and they will depend on your interpretation of the play.

② Continue the Scene

The three of them discuss their backgrounds and their likes and dislikes about school subjects.

Develop the Plot

Blair mentions something odd about the building. It seems as though they have all come a different way to Room 77. Something odd could happen now, perhaps to do with a sound or sounds and a light or lights. Blair might sneak a look on Miss Starr's desk.

③ Continue the Scene

They argue about the tunnel, the door, the escalator, the size of the building. They all seem to have entered a different building. Geoffrey could have had the feeling of going down rather than up.

Develop the Plot

Miss Starr discovers that they have been looking on her desk. She tells them off for interfering in matters that have already been decided. She may inform them that Mr Universe is aware of what they have done. How might they react to this?

④ Continue the Scene

They continue their discussion of the odd questions on the application form after Miss Starr and Geoffrey have gone. What questions might have appeared on this form?

Develop the Plot

They might ask Miss Starr some questions when she returns about the nature of the job and what Mr Universe is like. She could block these questions by answering with a question. Or her answers may be vague and mysterious.

Continue the Scene

They talk about Geoffrey and why they think he will, or will not, get the job.

Develop the Plot

Something else odd happens. It could be a strange noise. It could be the singing of a choir. They are uneasy. They discuss what they were doing before they came here. Hint at accidents, illnesses and so on, but be subtle. There could be some confusion and disagreement among them over the day and date.

 Continue the Scene

Samantha begins to panic. She hammers on the door. The others try to calm her.

Develop the Plot

On the other side of the room Miss Starr appears. She says nothing but looks at them. What could she do to build up the tension? She leaves without being seen but she could make a noise so they suspect that someone or something has been in the room. Again lighting and sound effects can be used to create the atmosphere you want.

⟨7⟩ Finish the Play

Decide by discussion whether this is the best cut-off point for the play to end. Add what you like but still leave the play a mystery. We do not feel that there should be explanations.

After your work on the play you might like to discuss whether the play would be improved by adding other characters, for instance a caretaker. We do not think Mr Universe should appear. What do you think?

The play is written for a bare stage with just furniture and a few properties. It would also make an interesting radio play with electronic music perhaps.

THE CONCERT

Characters in the play

Dave Watson, nearly 20
Mr Watson, Dave's father
Mrs Watson, his mother
Linda Watson, young teenager
Aunty Hazel, Mrs Watson's younger sister
Adam Chapman, age 24
Colin Blackley, age 20
Nick Sellars, age 19, friend of Colin
Barbara Wade, in charge of public address system
Manager, of the 'Silver Slipper' nightclub, middle aged

Characters for Scene One

Dave Watson   Linda Watson
Mr Watson   Aunty Hazel
Mrs Watson

Scene One The Watson's living room. The family are discussing **Dave**'s ambitions to become a pop musician.

Mr Watson He stays out too late, practising. Then he can't get up in the morning.
Mrs Watson He's not been late for work often.
Mr Watson Often enough. One of these days he'll lose that job.
Mrs Watson You worry too much.
Mr Watson And he doesn't worry enough. He can't think of anything but that pop group. Silly play-acting. He needs to keep his mind on his work.
Aunty Hazel What are they calling themselves now?

28

Mr Watson	'Danicade'. Ridiculous name.
Aunty Hazel	They've got to call themselves something.
Mrs Watson	There are a lot of groups with sillier names.
Linda	I've heard them and I think they're great.
Mr Watson	You would.
Hazel	You don't like any kind of music.
Mr Watson	I don't like their kind of music. It's just a flipping row to me.
Mrs Watson	Anyway, it gives him an interest.
Mr Watson	Does it? Gives 'em an excuse for a booze up more like.
Linda	That's not fair, Dad. They spend hours practising.
Mr Watson	So they say.
Hazel	You're just an old stick in the mud.
Mr Watson	Oh yes? Well, let me tell you, being an old stick in the mud has kept this family going for years and years.
Mrs Watson	You can see the attraction, though, can't you, Don? If they're a success?
Mr Watson	Our Dave? Fat chance of that.
Hazel	Don't be so mean.
Mr Watson	That's not mean. That's sense.
Linda	No, it isn't. You know nothing about it. That's stupid.
Mrs Watson	Linda!
Dave	(*Comes in*) Hello, Aunty Hazel. What's all this, then?
Mr Watson	Where've you been till this time?
Dave	With the group.
Mrs Watson	Have you had something to eat?
Dave	No, I mean – yes. It's all right, Mum. Er – Dad – can I ask you a favour?
Mr Watson	You can ask. What?
Dave	Can you lend me £150?
Mr Watson	£150?
Hazel	What for?

29

Dave	There's a Fender Telecaster guitar going second-hand. He only wants £150 for it.
Mrs Watson	You've got a guitar.
Dave	Yes. But the Fender's miles better than mine.
Mr Watson	£150? You must think I'm crackers.
Dave	But . . . well . . . Never mind, Dad. Forget I said it.
Mr Watson	Don't you worry. I will.
Hazel	Why do you need another guitar?
Dave	Well, we've got a gig booked at the Silver Slipper in a fortnight's time. It could be our big chance.
Linda	Hey, Dave! That's smashing!
Dave	The local paper will be there with a photographer and Adam's going to get a lot of support from 'Festival'.
Mr Watson	What festival?
Dave	It's another group, Dad. They're bringing a lot of their fans. Hiring a bus.
Mr Watson	Huh!
Mrs Watson	That's as maybe, Dave. But we can't lend you £150.
Hazel	Nor me. If I could, I would.
Mr Watson	Don't encourage him. It's all dreams. Pie in the sky. £150!
Dave	No. I understand. I'll make do with the guitar I've got, or I could . . .
Mr Watson	You could – what?
Dave	Nothing, Dad. I mean – there's something else.
Mrs Watson	If it's money . . . ?
Dave	No, it isn't money. But – you see – we've got several new songs I've written.
Mr Watson	Songs?
Dave	The thing is – we've nowhere to practise them.
Mrs Watson	I thought Adam was getting a place.

Dave It fell through, that did.
Mr Watson So?
Dave Adam was – we were – I was wondering if we could use our garage.
Mr Watson You what?

Characters for Scene Two

Dave   **Colin Blackley**
Adam Chapman   **Nick Sellars**

Scene Two The kitchen of **Adam**'s house. They are discussing the problem of finding a place to practise for the show.

Colin We're still twenty minutes short of a show.
Nick Right. Unless we find somewhere to practise, we're dead.
Dave But where?
Adam You're asking us?
Colin Yes, Dave. You've let us down.
Dave No, I haven't.
Colin You swore we'd be all right with the garage.
Dave How was I to know?
Adam You should have known.
Nick Ben Ramsay might give us a hand.
Adam How?
Nick He's got that uncle in Fallingford.
Colin That scrap merchant?
Nick Yes. He's got a big shed for the business, well away from the village.
Adam Is there electricity for the amps? You think he might let us use the shed?
Nick There's power laid on. Ben said he might be willing.
Colin Well let's get hold of Ben.

31

Nick There'd be a price. Ben said so. It means bringing him into the band.
Dave He doesn't know the numbers. He wouldn't have time to learn them.
Adam We don't need two backing guitars.
Nick No. But you know what Ben's like. We wouldn't get the shed unless we brought him in.
Dave What are you getting at, Nick?
Nick Nothing. I'm just saying what's what. That's all.
Dave You want to swap me for Ben Ramsay?
Adam Without Ben we've nowhere to practise.
Colin And if we don't get at least four nights' practice, we don't have a show.
Dave I've written a lot of our songs. I've put weeks into this gig already.
Adam So have we all.
Colin If we have to cancel now, the club will never give us another booking.
Dave Ben would never be able to learn the programme in time.
Nick He's pretty good. He might.
Adam I suppose we could have two rhythm guitars.
Colin But what would it sound like?
Adam It'd be different.
Nick But would it be better?
Dave Oh, come on! You want me to stand down? I thought we were mates.
Nick We are.
Colin We could at least try Ben in with us.
Nick No harm in that.
Adam Except – he'd want to play on the night, too, wouldn't he?
Dave Listen. I'll try again. I'll get us somewhere to practise.
Adam Where?
Dave My uncle in Warram's got a small-

	holding. There's a big shed or barn there.
Colin	You haven't said anything about him before.
Dave	I haven't seen him for some time.
Colin	You reckon there's a chance?
Adam	It's half an hour's run to Warram.
Dave	Oh, no. It's less. It's worth trying.
Adam	How are you going to get out there to ask?
Dave	Colin?
Colin	All right. I think I can borrow the van. But we need money for petrol.
Dave	I've got a couple of quid. Come on.

Characters for Scene Three

Nick   **Dave**
Adam   **Colin**

Scene Three *The kitchen in* **Adam**'s *house. About ten days later.*

Nick	It went well last night.
Adam	Well, it won't go well tonight unless Colin turns up soon with that van.
Dave	We're running very late. He could have let us know.
Nick	He'll be here in a minute.
Adam	You've been saying that for the last half hour.
Dave	Anyway.
Adam	Anyway – what?
Dave	We don't need to go through all the numbers again, do we. Just run over those new ones a couple of times more.
Adam	We won't have time to run through anything at this rate. Where is Colin?

Dave He's really let us down tonight.
Nick Oh, no he hasn't.
Dave Well – what do you call this?
Nick Just keep your hair on. He'll be coming.
Dave Will he? It's all right for him, isn't it? You went on enough about my not getting us anywhere to practise. But if Colin let's us down . . .
Nick He's not let us down.
Dave He's not here, is he?
Adam Pack it in, you two. Like a couple of kids.

(Colin comes in)

Adam Where the hell have you been?
Colin What do you mean? Where have I been? I've been trying to get us some transport, haven't I?
Nick What's up with the van?
Colin Wrecked.
Adam How?
Colin Going up and down the lane to that small-holding, I reckon. It packed up on Geoff this morning while he was delivering. In the garage for repairs.
Dave What do we do now?
Adam Well, we don't have this last practice for one thing.
Nick But we need another practice.
Colin We're not going to get one.
Adam Will the van be ready for Saturday?
Colin Search me.
Dave You're the one who ought to know.
Colin It doesn't make any difference whether I know or not.
Adam Course it does. How are we going to get all our stuff to the club without that van?
Colin Good question. We're not getting the van again.

Adam	Why not?
Colin	I've had a row with Geoff. He blames me for the damage. He won't lend me the van again.
Dave	We can't carry all that stuff down to the club.
Adam	We could do it in a couple of trips with your Dad's estate car.
Dave	He hasn't let me drive his car since I had that accident.
Adam	But that was nothing. Years ago.
Dave	It wasn't years. He hasn't forgotten.
Colin	You can ask him.
Nick	Tell him it's an emergency.
Dave	We could get a couple of taxis.
Nick	That would cost more than the club's paying us.
Dave	I know. All right. I'll ask him. But I know what he'll say.

3

Characters for Scene Four

Nick	Dave
Colin	Barbara Wade
Adam	Manager

Scene Four Backstage at the 'Silver Slipper' nightclub. The public address system is being set up.

Nick	I've never seen a girl rigging up a public address system before.
Colin	Does she know what she's doing?
Adam	Here she is.

(*Barbara comes in*)

Adam	Ask her.
Colin	Excuse me.
Barbara	Yes?

Colin There was a bit of feed back through one of the amps.
Barbara It's fixed.
Colin Oh, good.
Barbara This your first time?
Dave More or less.
Barbara Nervous?
Adam So-so.
Barbara You'll be all right once you're on.

(*Barbara goes*)

Nick There's a big crowd out there.
Dave I hope we go down well.
Adam They'll let us know if we don't.
Colin Not worried, are you?
Nick A bit.
Dave My hands are sweating.
Adam Mm. My throat's a bit dry.
Colin You should have had a couple of beers like me. I'm not worried. We'll be great.

(*Manager comes in*)

Manager Ready?
Adam Just about.
Manager You'll do your best, won't you, lads?
Dave We will.
Manager They can be a funny crowd here sometimes.
Nick In what way?
Manager Noisy, if they don't like you.
Adam Oh.
Manager I can always get you off the stage. Put the main group on early I suppose . . .
Nick You're expecting trouble?
Manager Oh, no. No. Forget it. Are you ready?
Adam We are.
Manager Good luck, then. You're on.
Colin Oh, God.

Work on the play

⟨1⟩ Continue the Scene

In spite of what the others say to persuade him, Mr Watson will not let Dave and the group use the garage for practice.

Develop the Plot

Mr Watson agrees after an argument. The neighbours on one side of the Watsons are the Kayes. The Watsons have often complained about the Kayes' dog damaging their garden. The Kayes and the Watsons are not very friendly. Mr Kaye is a talkative man. Mrs Kaye agrees with everything he says. On the other side of the Watsons are Bill and Vicki Dent. They are friends of the Watsons but they have Vicki's mother staying with them. She is ill and can't stand noise. Both sets of neighbours come to complain to the Watsons about the group practising and Mr Watson has to ban the group from the garage.

OR

An extra scene: Dave goes to see someone from the bank about an interview with the manager which he gets. Does he succeed in borrowing the money for the guitar?

⟨2⟩ Develop the Plot

It will be more effective if Dave and Colin have some trouble in persuading Dave's uncle and aunt. Invent names for these. You might bring in a cousin of Dave's, a girl, who is on his side. How long is it since these relations last saw Dave? Recently? A year? Several years? What objections might they raise? Would the noise frighten the animals? Is there electric power in their shed? If not could the group run a long lead from the house? Will the aunt and uncle charge for the electricity or the rent of the shed? Does Colin help or hinder Dave in his arguments? Discuss the possible reactions of Dave's relations and what might happen before they let the group practise. Then act out the scene.

Continue the Scene

Dave and Colin report back to Adam and Nick that they are going to be allowed to practise in Warram.

⟨3⟩ Develop the Plot

Is Mr Watson annoyed that Dave has been to relatives for help? Or is he pleased at Dave's initiative? Would Mrs Watson, Hazel and Linda argue that relatives have helped Dave more than his immediate family and make Mr Watson feel that he ought to be more sympathetic to the band? Or does his relations' attitude make Mr Watson angry and more opposed to Dave? Does Dave manage to borrow the car or not? Discuss what might happen.
Act out the scene, but remember that Dave and his friends do manage to arrange some transport in the end. What is it?

⟨4⟩ Finish the Play

Is the concert a complete failure? Do the group quarrel about it, blaming each other? Do they break up? Is there a scene in which we find out how Mr Watson feels about this?

OR

Is the concert neither a success nor a failure? Do we find this out when Dave discusses it later with his family? Is he disappointed? What does his father say?

OR

Is the concert a success and do we find this out immediately at the club? Does the manager offer them another booking? Does the newspaper offer to take free photographs of them to be used for publicity?

Has there been an agent or promoter at the concert who offers the possibility of further bookings elsewhere? Discuss what might happen, creating further characters, if necessary, and then act out the final scene or scenes.

BOAT TRIP

Characters in the play

Caroline Foster, teenager
Tony, her brother
Eve Weston teenager
Becky, her sister
Greg White, teenager
Sarah, his sister
Roger Newton, cousin of Caroline and Tony, age about 22
Terry Barnes, a radio reporter (voice only)
Radio Announcer (voice only)
Mr Weston, Eve and Becky's father
Mr White, Greg and Sarah's father
Mrs White, Greg and Sarah's mother
Mr Foster, Caroline and Tony's father
Mrs Foster, Caroline and Tony's mother
Brant, a man in his 20s
Alec, about the same age as Brant
Lena, a woman in her early 20s
Police Sergeant
Police Inspector

Characters for Scene One

Caroline Foster
Tony Foster
Eve Weston
Becky Weston
Greg White
Sarah White
Roger Newton
Terry Barnes
Radio Announcer

Scene One The teenagers are all on holiday with their parents. **Roger** has taken them out to sea in a small boat. The engine has stopped. **Caroline** is listening to a small radio.

Roger   I can't get this engine going again. We'll have to row.

Radio   This is Radio Seastrand with

	Afternoon Report. Police are still searching for two men and a woman who carried out a jewel robbery in Horkham earlier today. Terry Barnes reports:
Eve	Oh, get something else. That's boring. Get some music.
Terry Barnes	Mr Benson, the shop manager told me today that two men and a woman came into his shop at about ten this morning. They first asked to see some rings . . .
Becky	Horkham? That's not far away. We went there last Saturday.
Roger	Turn it off. It's giving me a headache. And we've got to get moving before the tide turns.
Caroline	All right. (*She switches the radio off*)
Tony	Horkham's only about ten miles away.
Greg	If I had my CB radio we'd be all right.
Eve	Well, you haven't. And how would we be all right? Stupid.
Sarah	Why stupid? If we could call up the shore, they'd send another boat out.
Tony	And tow us in.
Roger	Never mind about all that. Who's going to row first?
Eve	I can't row.
Becky	Nor me.
Roger	I'd better be the one to steer. I feel rotten, anyway.
Caroline	I'll have a go. Sarah?
Sarah	I'll try.
Tony	You row for a bit. Then me and Greg will take over.
Greg	Right.

1

41

> *Characters for Scene Two*
>
> | | |
> |---|---|
> | Caroline | Eve |
> | Roger | Becky |
> | Tony | Sarah |
> | Greg | |

Scene Two The boat has arrived at the beach of a small bay on an island.

Eve   Oh, come on! We're not staying here, are we?
Greg   Moan! Moan! Moan! Why don't you shut up?
Roger   We have to stop here, Eve. Everybody's tired out. We can't row against the tide.
Tony   And I'm getting blisters on my hands. Look!
Greg   Eve can't be tired out.
Eve   What do you know about it? I wish I'd never come on this rotten trip.
Caroline   Can't you try to get the motor going, Roger?
Roger   Impossible. I think something's seized.
Sarah   What do you mean – seized?
Greg   He means bust, our kid.
Eve   Well – what are we going to do now? Just sit here in this boat like dummies?
Roger   No. Take this line ashore and tie us up.
Eve   Me? I'll get my feet wet.
Caroline   Give it here, Rodge. (*She takes the line, wades ashore and ties up the boat*)
Roger   Right. Now we won't drift away. So – the rest of you – out!
Eve   That water's deep.
Roger   Oh, do stop whingeing, Eve. I've got a blinding headache.
Tony   It isn't deep. (*Gets out of the boat*) See! No problem. (*Wades ashore*)

Eve	I hate getting these trainers wet. They feel so nasty.
Greg	(*Getting out and making for shore*) Well, take 'em off, you twit.
Becky	How long are we stopping here? We won't be here all night, will we?

(*They begin to get out of the boat*)

Roger	We can't even try to get back until the tide turns again. They might have come looking for us before that. Come on, Eve. Out!
Greg	Do you want a hand, Sarah? There are some slippery rocks here.
Sarah	No. I'll be all right.
Eve	It's cold. This water's freezing.
Becky	And these rocks are dangerous. I could fall.
Tony	Come on, Becky. I'll give you a hand.

(*They all reach the sand*)

Eve	Where are we? Are there any shops? I'm hungry.
Greg	Oh yes. Millions of shops Eve. Look.
Eve	Oh, you are so clever, Greg, aren't you?
Roger	Pack it in, you two. We aren't far from the mainland. Look. (*He draws on the sand*) That's the mainland. And this is the island where we are.
Becky	Well, if it isn't far, why can't we row back there?
Caroline	The tide will be against us now, Roger, won't it?
Roger	That's right. It'd be too dangerous to chance it. I don't think any of us have the strength to row against it.
Tony	What shall we do, then?
Roger	See that track?
Greg	Yes?
Becky	Where? What track?

43

Sarah	Running up the hill. There!
Becky	Oh, yes.
Eve	It looks dangerous to me.
Roger	No, it isn't. Just over the top there are two cottages. We'll go there.
Caroline	Do you think they'll have a boat?
Greg	We've got a boat.
Caroline	I mean one with a motor.
Roger	Maybe. They might have a phone.
Eve	We don't all have to go, do we?
Roger	Yes. We'll stick together. Come on. Oh, dear. I really do feel bad. Go on. I'll follow slowly.

‹2›

> Characters for Scene Three
>
> **The same** as in Scene Two

Scene Three	**Caroline** *is leading on the track up the hill with the others following.* **Roger** *is a long way behind the rest.*
Tony	(*Just behind* **Caroline**) What's the hold up? Out of breath?
Caroline	No. Look down there. Roger. He's just tripped over.
Eve	I said this path was dangerous.
Sarah	He's not getting up.
Greg	Yes, he is.
Tony	No, he isn't. He's just slumped down again on that rock.
Sarah	He must have hurt himself.
Caroline	We'd better see. Down we go again.
Becky	All that way back again?
Eve	We don't all have to go. I'll stay here.
Becky	So will I.

(**Becky** *and* **Eve** *stay where they are. The others go back*)

Caroline	What's the matter, Roger? Are you all right?
Roger	No. It's this rotten migraine. It's been coming on all afternoon. I feel sick. I can't see too well.
Tony	Why didn't you say?
Roger	No point. There's nothing anyone can do about it.
Sarah	You really ought to be lying down in a darkened room. That helps.
Greg	Brilliant idea. Where is this darkened room, Sarah?
Sarah	I was only saying.
Caroline	Can't you walk?
Roger	I'll be all right in a minute. I stumbled on one of these blasted stones in the path.
Tony	Did you hurt yourself?
Roger	I went down on my ankle and twisted it. That's why I had to sit down. Let me get up. Aah! (*He tries to stand but is forced to sit down again*)
Caroline	We'll help you. You can lean on us.
Sarah	Yes. You take that side, Caroline. I'll support him on this.
Tony	No. It's better if me and Greg do it.
Roger	Don't bother. It'll be a struggle getting up this narrow path. We could all have a tumble. Listen. The cottage is just over the top of the hill. You can't miss it.
Tony	Are you sure?
Roger	Yes.
Caroline	You'd be better off in the shade of that rock just back there. Can you make it, if we help you?
Roger	No. Just leave me.
Caroline	You ought to have someone staying with you.

⟨3⟩

45

Characters for Scene Four

Mr Weston   Mr Foster
Mr White   Mrs Foster
Mrs White

Scene Four In a caravan on a seaside caravan park. All the parents, except Mrs Weston, are discussing the late return of the boat.

Mrs White	Do you think they're all right?
Mr Foster	Why shouldn't they be?
Mr Weston	They are a bit overdue.
Mrs Foster	I can't see the boat any more from this window.
Mr White	No. It's gone out of sight behind the island.
Mrs White	Behind the island? Why have they gone round the island?
Mr White	Don't ask me.
Mrs Foster	I thought they were coming straight back.
Mr Foster	They'll be all right. Just gone to take a look, I reckon. Roger knows what he's doing.
Mrs Foster	Roger? Does he? Are you sure about that?
Mr White	It's been a fine sunny day. The sea's calm. I don't think there's much to worry about.
Mr Weston	It is getting a bit late, though.
Mrs White	Do you think we should do something?
Mr Foster	Such as?
Mrs White	Well – tell someone.
Mr White	Who?
Mrs Foster	The coastguard?
Mr White	The coastguard! Tell him what? That they've gone on a boat trip?

Mrs White	Perhaps we should.
Mr White	And have the lifeboat out, eh?
Mrs Foster	I don't know.
Mr Foster	On a day like this? I don't think they can be in any danger.
Mr White	No. The lifeboat's a bit extreme, isn't it?
Mrs Foster	Hm. Perhaps you're right.

4

Characters for Scene Five

Brant	Eve
Alec	Becky
Lena	Caroline
Greg	Tony

Scene Five   The cottage. All the teenagers, except Sarah, are there.

Brant	What are you all doing here? What do you want?
Greg	We want to get back to the mainland.
Eve	Our stupid boat has broken down.
Greg	And it's too dangerous to row back. The tide's too strong.
Eve	We're wet and hungry. Are there any shops near here?
Alec	(*Comes into the room*) Who are you? What's going on?
Caroline	We need help. We were on a boat trip. The engine broke down.
Lena	Where's the boat now?
Tony	On the beach at the bottom of the path.
Alec	Someone passing might start nosing around. Brant – go down and take a look at it.

Brant   Right.

(**Brant** *goes quickly out*)

Becky   Have you got a phone here?
Lena   No.
Eve   Well, is there any way you can get us back to the mainland?
Lena   We'll have to see.
Alec   Who knows you're here?
Tony   No one. We ended up here by accident.
Greg   Our parents know we're out in a boat.
Alec   When do they expect you back?
Caroline I think we really should have been back by now.
Lena   Where are your parents?
Tony   On the caravan site. Haverness Clifftop Caravan Site.
Lena   Where's that?
Caroline On the mainland. You can see it from the other side of the island, I think.
Alec   Will they be out looking for you?
Greg   Not if we can get back to the mainland before it's dark. So we need help.
Alec   You do, do you?
Eve   Is that a lot to ask? You're not being very helpful.
Lena   Sorry, kids. It's just that – er –
Alec   We're just surprised to see you. Taken aback. No one comes here, you see.
Lena   We like it because it's quiet. One of us has been ill.
Alec   That's it. Brant. He needs peace and quiet. Rest.
Lena   We're looking after him.
Caroline Oh. We're sorry to be a nuisance, then.
Lena   Yes. Well. (*There is a short silence*)
Alec   Sit down, all of you. Lena, come into the other room. (*To the teenagers*) I'm not sure what we can do.

Lena   We'll have to discuss it. You stay here.

(**Lena** and **Alec** go out)

Eve   What weird people!
Becky   I don't like them.
Greg   Why not?
Becky   I just don't.
Greg   That's daft.
Becky   No, it isn't.
Caroline   They are a bit edgy. I wonder . . . ? No.

(**Brant** comes in)

Brant   Alec! Where's Alec? Where are they?
Caroline   Talking in the other room.

(**Alec** comes in)

Alec   Well?
Brant   There's a boat there all right. You can see it from the hilltop.
Alec   And?
Brant   No sweat. It's out of sight of the mainland. But there's a man and a kid down there on the path.
Alec   Is there? You'd better go and bring them both up here.
Caroline   Roger won't be able to get up here without help.
Brant   Roger? He's with you?
Greg   Yes. He's hurt his leg. He can't walk.
Alec   Come on. We'll both go down and take a look at him.
Brant   How about these kids?

(**Lena** comes in)

Alec   Lena can look after them, can't you, Lena?
Lena   Yes. I'll see they . . . I'll look after them.
Alec   Let's go.

(**Alec** and **Brant** leave)

Caroline Where's the bathroom, please?
Lena What? Oh, yes. Through that door. Up the stairs. It's facing you.
Caroline Thanks.

(**Caroline** *goes out*)

Eve Are you sure there isn't a telephone somewhere around here?
Lena Dead sure. We're completely cut off.
Greg How do you get to the mainland?
Lena By boat.
Greg Where is it now?
Lena Making a trip.
Tony When will it be back?
Lena Don't worry. We expect it back quite soon. It'll take you then.
Eve But how soon?
Lena I can't say exactly. Soon enough.
Eve My Mum will be worried.
Tony Isn't there some way we can signal to the mainland?
Lena No. No way at all.
Tony What if we went up to the top of that next hill outside?
Greg Yes. We could light a fire up there. Wave something.
Becky Ooh, yes. Good idea.
Lena You mustn't do that.
Greg Why not?
Lena It's dangerous to go up there. Where's that pal of yours got to? I'd better go and look.

(**Caroline** *comes in*)

I was wondering where you'd got to.
Caroline I've been to the front door. Your friends are calling for you.
Lena What? I didn't hear anything.
Caroline I saw them waving from the landing window. I went down and opened the front door. I could hardly hear them

	from there but there's a boat coming round the island.
Lena	What! A boat! What sort of a boat?
Caroline	Just a boat. Shall I go and see what they want?
Lena	No, you will not. You all stay here.

(**Lena** *hurries out*)

Caroline	Big trouble! These are the people who did that jewel robbery.
Becky	Oh, no! How d'you know? Oh, whatever are we going to do?
Caroline	I was suspicious so I had a snoop round upstairs.
Tony	But what did you find?
Caroline	Two empty bags with a jeweller's name in them! They were partly hidden under a bed. A bit was sticking out.
Tony	Empty?
Caroline	Yes. There were empty jeweller's trays, too. And a couple of new handbags.
Greg	What was in those?
Caroline	I only had time for a quick look. I daren't stay up there long and one bag was locked. The other had rings and brooches and banknotes in it.
Eve	We've got to get out of here. Hide somewhere outside.
Caroline	They'd soon find us. I had a look in the kitchen. They've got a two-way radio there.
Greg	Have they? I'll bet I can use it. Come on and show me (*Going*)
Tony	Hang on, Greg. Was there a boat? Was there someone shouting out there?
Caroline	No. I said that to get her out of the way.
Tony	Then she'll be back any second. We

Greg	won't have time to get the radio working. I know. We'll send her off again.
Greg	How?
Tony	Two of us will slip out before she can get back. Tell her we've gone to signal the mainland from the top of that hill.
Caroline	Yes. She'll be dead scared in case anyone from the mainland spots that they're here. She'll go after you.
Tony	You come with me, Eve.
Eve	No fear. What if she catches us? You don't know what she might do to us.
Becky	I'll go with you.
Caroline	Go out the back door. She'll be coming in the front way.
Tony	Right.

(**Tony** and **Becky** go out)

Caroline	I just hope you can work that radio, Greg.
Greg	Trust me.

5

Characters for Scene Six

Lena   Greg
Caroline Eve

Scene Six A few minutes later. **Greg**, **Caroline** and **Eve** are in the room. **Lena** hurries in angrily.

Lena	Just what is your game, kid? No one was calling me. There was no boat.
Caroline	I'm sure I heard someone calling.
Lena	Where are those other two?
Greg	Oh, they've gone.
Lena	Gone? What the hell do you mean?

Caroline	They've gone to try to signal to the mainland.
Lena	They've what . . . ? Where?
Greg	They've gone to the top of the hill.
Caroline	Tony said he was going to wave his shirt or start a fire or something.
Greg	He was hoping it could be seen from the cliff on the mainland.
Lena	The little . . . ! You stay here. Right where you are. Otherwise you're in trouble. I mean that. Very serious trouble. Got it?
Caroline	Yes. But I don't understand.
Lena	Don't try. Just stay right here or you'll be sorry.

(**Lena** *goes out*)

Caroline	Listen!
Greg	She's running.
Caroline	She's gone. (*She tries to open the door*) She's locked this door.
Greg	(*Tries to open the window*) This window's jammed. Stuck. It won't give. I'll smash it.
Caroline	No. She might hear the noise and come back. The key's still in this lock outside the door. I can see it through the keyhole. Try that small top window.
Greg	Right. Yes. This one will open. But it's too small for me to get through. Or for you.
Caroline	Eve could get through it.
Eve	No, no! Not me! I'm scared. I might fall and hurt myself.
Caroline	No, you won't. (*Grabs her*) Come on, Greg. Give me a hand to lift her up.
Eve	(*Struggling*) No. Leave me alone.
Greg	(*Also holding her*) Stop it, you fool. You've got to.
Caroline	Yes. You've got to get help. Think of

Eve	what she'll do if she comes back knowing we've tricked her.
Eve	(*Going through the window*) Help! I'm stuck. I told you this'd happen!
Caroline	You're not stuck. On you go.
Eve	I can't. I can't. You're hurting me!
Caroline	You can. One last shove, Greg.
Greg	Right. There you are, Eve. See! Easy!
Eve	(*Outside*) What do I do now?
Greg	Honestly!
Caroline	Come back inside the house and unlock this door, you gump.

(**Eve** *goes*)

Greg	Give me strength! Some people! I only hope she doesn't just whizz off in a panic.
Caroline	She's scared.
Greg	She's thick.
Caroline	She's coming. I can hear her.
Eve	(*Opening the door*) There! I've done it!

6

Characters for Scene Seven

Police Sergeant   Greg
Police Inspector   Eve
Caroline

Scene Seven *Outside the cottage. The* **Sergeant** *and* **Inspector** *are with the teenagers. The* **Sergeant** *is talking over a hand radio.*

Sergeant	Yes. Yes. I've got that. You have the three prisoners and the proceeds of the robbery. Good. (*To* **Inspector**) They've got 'em, sir.
Inspector	Splendid. And you kids are all right?
Caroline	Yes. Fine.

Inspector	Who called us up?
Greg	Me. But it was Caroline's idea.
Inspector	You did well.
Eve	They couldn't have done it without me.
Greg	You? You were scared rotten.
Caroline	Oh, shut up, Greg. We'd still be in that room, if it wasn't for Eve.
Greg	Yes. Okay. You're not so bad, Eve.
Eve	Oh, thanks very much, I'm sure.
Inspector	That about wraps it up. You stay here, Sergeant. I'll send someone to relieve you.
Sergeant	Right, sir.
Inspector	I imagine you lot don't want to stop here, too, do you?
Greg	Not likely.
Eve	I'm hungry.
Caroline	So am I. Starving.
Inspector	Off we go, then. Soon have you home. We'll pick up the others on the way.

7

Work on the play

1. Continue the Scene

Does the rowing go smoothly? Or do Caroline and Sarah turn out to be very bad at it? Are Tony and Greg any better? Do they all find it very hard work? Do Eve and Becky refuse to help at all? Is there a quarrel? Does Roger have to take over? Does the exertion make him feel worse? Do Tony and Greg have to come to the rescue? Discuss what might happen on the way to the island and then act out the scene.

Develop the Plot

The three jewel thieves are two men called Alec and Brant and a woman called Lena. They have made their getaway to a house on the island. They talk about how much the stolen jewels will be worth and how clever they have been in making a clean getaway.

② Develop the Plot

Is Caroline right or does Roger insist that they all go? What arguments might he use? That it will be safer to go and get someone from the cottage to come down to him? A couple of adults will be stronger than the teenagers? It will be easier, if they phone for a boat, for Roger to get back down to the beach than it will be for him to go on climbing to the top of the hill? Are they easily convinced or do they argue? You will see that we have decided that Sarah stays with him. Why might this be? She knows something about migraine. Does she know about first-aid? Is she just the kindest of them all? Is she the most fond of Roger? Discuss and act out the rest of the scene.

OR

The thieves are waiting in the cottage. They are slightly anxious. A boat, piloted by another member of the gang is waiting across the Channel. Under cover of night, it will come across to take them and their loot to the Continent. They have a radio with them so that they can contact the boat, if there is a hitch in their plans. Are they British crooks or are there some foreign members of the gang? Have they done only this robbery? Or is there the loot from several robberies hidden in the house? Discuss how much of this they might talk about among themselves and then act out their conversation and their plans.

OR

An extra scene: you might like to bring in a scene showing how close the police are to catching the thieves. Are they completely baffled? Are they looking for the thieves on the mainland? Do they suspect the gang are still in the area? They will have to set up road blocks and will be receiving reports from these. Do they also have a boat patrolling the coast to cut off escape that way? If you decide to do this scene, you will have to discuss how many characters you will need and their rank. It will probably be best to set it in police headquarters. There will be more suspense in the play if the police are not too close behind the gang.

③ Develop the Plot

At this stage you can decide either to go straight on to the next scene or to develop this one. Mrs Weston might come in at this point. Is she a rather fussy person like her daughter, Eve? Does she claim that the others are not taking matters seriously enough? Do they calm her down or does she make them anxious, too? What time was the boat supposed to get back? What time is it now? What other reasons might there be for the parents to grow anxious? Where – if they decide to – do they look for help – the coastguard or the police?

④ Develop the Plot

Extra scenes: these two are not vital to the play as we can imagine what is happening but you might like to discuss whether to expand the play by including them.

(a) What do Alec and Lena talk about when they leave the teenagers alone? Obviously they do not have much time to decide to pretend to be innocent people staying on the island. What else might they decide? Are they made so anxious by the presence of the children that they radio the boat and ask it to come at once and not wait for dark? Is this what Lena has been doing when she comes in after Alex? Or has she not had sufficient time?

(b) What do Alec and Brant and Roger and Sarah talk about? Is Roger willing to be helped up the path to the cottage where the crooks can keep a better watch on him? Or, feeling even more ill, does he decide to stay where he is? If so, would they use force on him to get him to the cottage? Or would that give the game away and tell him who they really were? You might think about this from the point of view of the thieves. Is it more sensible to leave Roger where he is with Brant staying with him? What would you do, if you were Alec or Brant?

⟨5⟩ Develop the Plot

The next scene is in the kitchen. Greg summons help with the radio. Does he get through at once or does he have difficulty? Do Caroline and Eve make helpful or unhelpful suggestions? Do they contact the police? Or is there a boat out already, looking for them? Did their parents contact the police or the coastguard after all? (See ⟨3⟩, Develop the Plot, page 57.) Do the thieves come back and catch them? Do they lock the teenagers up again and make their escape? How? Have they a boat to take them back to the mainland for escape that way? Or does the boat from the Continent arrive and pick them up? Or do the teenagers finish their radio message and escape from the house to hide on the island?

⟨6⟩ Finish the Play

We have deliberately left out the details of the climax of the play, the capture of the criminals, because there are several possibilities you might like to develop in a scene or scenes. They must, of course, depend on what has happened before in the play. You will also have to discuss how many characters you are going to bring in for the scene or scenes.

Does Lena bring back Tony and Becky in time to find out what Greg, Caroline and Eve have been doing? How? Does she have a gun? Do Alec and Brant see the police coming and try to use Roger's damaged boat for a getaway? Could Roger and Sarah stop them? Or would they not try? Or, do Alec and Brant dash back to the cottage for their loot and try to get away in the boat they have summoned from across the Channel? If you put in 'Extra Scene (a)' at the end of Scene Five, (see ④, Develop the Plot, page 57) what you did there might dictate what you improvise here. There are other possibilities for action which you might like to think up. Discuss these and act them out.

LET'S HAVE A PARTY

―――Characters in the play―――
Hazel Harbin, married but separated from her husband
Phil, her boyfriend
Chrissie, a friend of Hazel's
Nev, Chrissie's boyfriend
Carol, who comes to the party
Frankie, a friend of Carol's
Lee, Frankie's boyfriend
Mike, a neighbour of Hazel's
Nick, a friend of Hazel's
Liz, Nick's girlfriend
Cliff, a friend of Lee's
Wayne, also a friend of Lee's

―――Characters for Scene One―――
Hazel Harbin   Chrissie
Phil   Nev

Scene One *Hazel's flat.* **Hazel's** *baby Nicola is asleep in the room.* **Phil, Chrissie** *and* **Nev** *are there as well.* **Hazel** *has just finished answering the phone.*

Hazel He won't come and babysit. Isn't that just like my ex-husband? No wonder I left him. He says he's busy tonight.
Chrissie Doing what?
Hazel How should I know? Rotten swine.
Nev How about asking your Mum?
Hazel My Mum's up in Leicester staying with my sister.
Phil Well, don't get into a state. Who do you usually get if you want a baby-sitter?

Hazel	Carol came last time. Chrissie could you do it?
Chrissie	Oh, well – I suppose I could.
Nev	Why does it have to be Chrissie? We're going to that party tonight.
Chrissie	It's all right, Nev. I'll do it.
Hazel	I've got to go to this interview. I reckon I can get that receptionist's job and I need the money. I've got to try for it.
Nev	Hang on a minute. I've had an idea. We can have the party here.
Hazel	Oh, can you? Who says?
Phil	We'd have to bring over all the stuff from my place.
Nev	So? It's not all that far.
Phil	No. But there's a lot of it.
Nev	There's not all that much. There's only food and drink. We can get hold of some cardboard boxes and pack it all in there.
Phil	There's the stereo to bring.
Nev	No there isn't. We can use Hazel's.
Hazel	Hang on, hang on. Who said I'd let any of you lot muck around with my stereo?
Chrissie	Look. I don't mind. You have your party as planned. I'll just come here and babysit.
Nev	No, you won't. Why can't we have the party here? It's the perfect solution.
Hazel	Oh is it?
Nev	Of course it is. I don't see why Chrissie should miss a party just because you want to be off gallivanting about this evening.
Hazel	I'm not gallivanting about. I'm going for a job interview.
Nev	In the evening?
Hazel	Yes. In the evening. The hotel

Phil	manager couldn't fit me in at any other time. Do you think I wanted to go in the evening and leave Nicola? Look. I don't know what you two are getting so excited about. Chrissie's said that . . .
Nev	I know what Chrissie's said and I'm not having it. She's as much right to go to a party as anyone else. If Hazel wants to go out tonight, let her find her own baby-sitter.
Chrissie	No. It's all right, Nev. I'll stay here. I don't mind really.
Nev	Well, I do. You're always letting people take advantage of you.
Chrissie	No, I'm not.
Nev	Yes, you are. If Hazel wants someone to look after little Nicola, then we'll all look after her.
Hazel	While you're having a party? With all the racket going on? You must be joking.
Phil	It's not a bad idea, though, Hazel. We've had the stereo on in the evenings before and Nicola has slept through. If we have the party here, she's going to be well looked after.
Hazel	Oh, is she? You'll all be too busy enjoying yourselves to think about her.
Nev	No, we won't.

⟨1⟩

> *Characters for Scene Two*
>
> **Phil** **Frankie**
> **Chrissie** **Lee**
> **Nev** **Mike**
> **Carol**

Scene Two Hazel's *flat, a few hours later. The party is nearly ready to start.* **Phil, Chrissie** *and* **Nev** *are arranging things.* **Carol** *is with them.*

Carol Where did you put the orange? I can't see it in any of the boxes.
Phil It's in the kitchen. It needs making up with water. You'll find a big jug in the cupboard over the sink.
Carol Right.

(**Carol** *goes out*)

Nev Where's the baby?
Chrissie She's in the bedroom. Asleep. I've just looked.
Nev She'll be no bother.
Chrissie We'll have to keep an eye on her, though.

(*There is a knock at the door*)

Chrissie Who's that? They're not here already, are they?
Nev Why ask me? Go and see.

(**Chrissie** *opens the door to* **Mike**)

Mike Oh. Er – is Mrs Harbin in? I'm from the flat upstairs.
Chrissie Mrs Harbin?
Nev (*Coming to the door*) He means Hazel, you gump. No, I'm sorry, she's out. Gone for a job interview. We're some friends of hers. Can I help you?

Mike	Oh no, I don't think so. I heard noises down here and I just wondered...
Nev	Would you like to come in?
Chrissie	We're just getting ready for a party.
Mike	A party? Oh. No, thanks. Sorry I bothered you. (*He goes*)
Carol	(*Comes in*) Who was that?
Nev	Some bloke.
Carol	What did he want?
Nev	No idea. It sounded to me as if he lived upstairs.
Carol	It'd be Mike Westlake, then. He was in here one night, having coffee with Hazel when I came.
Phil	What's he like?
Carol	All right. Quiet. Steady.
Phil	Is he? Did you see the look on his face when Chrissie said we were having a party? He'll be down.
Nev	Well, if he is, we'll ask him in. That should settle it.
Phil	It's another good reason for keeping things on an even keel tonight. Remember what Hazel said. She doesn't want to come back here to chaos.
Nev	Oh, stop worrying. Listen. (*The baby is crying*)
Chrissie	That's Nicola. I'll go and see what the matter is.

(**Chrissie** *goes out into the bedroom*)

Nev	How's it going?
Carol	All ready out in the kitchen.
Nev	Right. Let's have some music then. They'll be here any minute now. (*He goes over to the stereo and puts on a tape*)
Phil	Keep it down, Nev.
Nev	Keep it down? You can hardly hear it. (*There is another knock at the door*)

	That'll be them. I'll get it.
	(**Nev** *opens the door and* **Lee** *and* **Frankie** *come in*)
Frankie	Hello, everybody. I've brought Lee along. I hope you don't mind.
Lee	And I've brought a bottle. (*He holds it up*)
Nev	We don't mind. The more the merrier.
Phil	What would you like to drink, Frankie?
Frankie	Oh, a soft drink for me.
Phil	Orange?
Frankie	That would be fine.
Lee	Not for me, mate. I'd like a real drink. Got any whisky?
Phil	I think so. It's out in the kitchen. Nev! Carol! Can you give me a hand out here?
	(**Phil** *goes into the kitchen and* **Nev** *and* **Carol** *follow*)
Nev	What do you want us in here for?
Phil	Gatecrashers. That bloke Lee wasn't invited. He could be trouble.
Carol	He's all right. He came with Frankie.
Phil	He's not all right. You may not know him but I do. He was at Bob Scobie's party a week or so ago and he was as drunk as a rat. He could be a disaster. He wants watching.
Nev	Oh, stop moaning, Phil. He'll be all right.
Carol	We can't throw him out now he's here, can we?
Phil	No. But we can make sure he's the only one uninvited.
Nev	Can we? What if Liz brings along someone we don't know? Talk sense. What are you going to do if you don't know someone? Ask 'em for their passport?

65

Phil Don't be daft.
Nev It's you that's being daft.
Carol No he isn't. I've been to a couple of parties that were ruined by gatecrashers. We don't want a lot of that tonight.
Phil No we don't. We said we'd look after this place. We don't want to be letting a lot of drunken yobbos in.
Nev Well – what do you suggest we do?

2

Characters for Scene Three

Phil	Nick
Chrissie	Liz
Nev	Cliff
Lee	Wayne

Scene Three *In the Living Room of* **Hazel**'s *flat. The party is in full swing.* **Liz** *and* **Nick** *have arrived and are talking to* **Chrissie** *in a corner of the room. Music is playing loudly. A couple are dancing.*

Nick Enjoying it, Chris?
Chrissie Not much.
Liz Why not?
Chrissie It's that baby. She keeps crying. I can't get her off to sleep again.
Liz Oh, babies always cry. Have you tried giving her a bottle with something sweet in it?
Nick I'm not surprised she can't sleep. Nev has got that stereo blasting away full bore. Shall I go and ask him to turn it down.
Liz Try it. See if that will get her off.
Nick Right. (*He goes over to* **Nev**)
Chrissie You come and have a look at her, Liz. You're a nurse.

Liz	I'm not. I'm still just a trainee.
Chrissie	Come anyway. You'll know more about it than I do.
Liz	Don't count on it.

(**Liz** and **Chrissie** *go out*)

Lee	(*Comes over to where* **Nick** *and* **Nev** *are talking*) What have you turned the music down for?
Nev	There's a baby in the other room. It's keeping her awake.
Lee	Babies don't mind a bit of row. I know. I'm an uncle. (*Turns the music up again*)
Nick	Turn it down!
Lee	Gerroff. (*He stops* **Nick** *getting to the stereo.* **Nev** *turns it down*) Hey, you, leave it on.
Nev	There's someone at the door. (*Goes to the door*)
Lee	I know who that'll be.
Nev	(*Opens the door*) What do you want? (*He blocks the way but we can see* **Cliff** *and* **Wayne** *there*)
Cliff	Lee! We found you.
Wayne	Let us in.
Nev	You're half cut.
Phil	(*Comes across*) What's going on?
Cliff	We've come to your party.
Phil	Oh, no, you haven't. You're not coming in here.
Wayne	Lee! They won't let us in.
Lee	(*Comes over*) Let 'em in. They're mates of mine.
Phil	Maybe. But I'm supposed to be looking after this flat. Look at them. They're not coming in here.

◇3◇

67

┌─────────── Characters for Scene Four ───────────┐
│   Phil   Liz   │
│   Chrissie   Nick   │
│   Nev   Mike   │
│   Carol   │
└──┘

Scene Four   *In the Living Room. The party is still going, although not as noisily as at first.*

Nev   You see? No problem. We got rid of them. Let's have some music. (*He turns it up again*)

Chrissie   (*Comes in from the bedroom*) Phil. Phil! (*She has to shout over the sound of the music*)

Phil   What? Turn that down, Nev. I can't hear what Chrissie wants.

Nev   You what?

Phil   (*Shouting*) Turn it down!

Nev   Oh! Right. (*He turns the sound down*)

Phil   What's up?

Chrissie   It's the baby. She keeps crying. And she's been sick twice. Liz is with her. She's worried, too.

Phil   Well, don't ask me. I don't know anything about babies.

Nev   I'll go and have a look at her.

(**Nev** *goes out*)

Chrissie   She hasn't been to sleep at all yet. She keeps trying to doze off and then she wakes up.

Phil   Isn't there something you can give her? Some medicine or something?

Chrissie   Such as what?

Phil   I don't know. Carol?

Carol   Yes?

Phil   Your sister's little boy is about the same age as Nicola, isn't he?

Carol   Yes.
Phil   And you look after him from time to time?
Carol   That's right.
Phil   Well, go and have a look at Nicola. Chrissie says she's not very well.
Carol   All right. But I'm no expert.

(**Carol** *goes out to the bedroom. People continue to enjoy themselves. Then* **Chrissie, Liz, Carol** *and* **Nev** *return.* **Chrissie** *is carrying the baby, Nicola*)

Nev   Turn the music down, will you, someone.
Phil   What's the matter? Is she bad?

(*Someone turns the music down*)

Liz   I think she's rather ill.
Chrissie   A doctor would be the best idea.
Nick   Who is her doctor? Does anyone know?
Chrissie   No.
Carol   I've no idea.
Phil   We'd better ring Hazel.
Liz   Where is she?
Nick   Which hotel has she gone to?
Chrissie   The Cumberland, I think.
Carol   Are you sure? I thought she said the Clifton.
Nev   Right. We'll ring both of them.
Carol   And what if we've got it wrong? Doesn't anyone know where she's gone?
Phil   Are you sure it wasn't the Carlton?
Nev   Well, we'll ring round them all.
Liz   It's just wasting time. What if she's on her way home? And what can she do when she gets here? This baby needs a doctor.
Nick   Well, let's stop pratting about and take her to a doctor.

Phil Yes. I'll ring for a taxi.

(*There is a knock at the door*)

Nev If that's those yobbos...!
Phil The last thing we need. Get rid of them.
Nev Right. (*He goes to the door*)
Chrissie We've tried giving her drinks but she brought it all back again.
Nev (*Opens door.* **Mike** *is there*) Yes?
Mike Is Mrs Harbin back?
Nev No. What do you want?
Mike It's a bit noisy. I was just wondering if you could ... er ... um ...
Nev Noisy? We've just turned it down.
Phil Nev! It's Mike, isn't it?
Mike Yes.
Phil Come in. (**Mike** *does so*) Could you help us?
Mike Help you?
Phil Do you have a car?
Mike Yes. Why?
Phil The baby's ill.
Mike Nicola?
Phil We want to get her to a doctor. We were just going to ring for a taxi but it might take some time to get here.
Nick None of us have a car here. We thought with having a party and drinking and all that...
Mike I'll take her.
Nick Where? We don't know who her doctor is. Do you know?
Mike No. I'm sorry.
Chrissie We'll just have to look in the phone book and ring any doctor we can find.
Liz We can't go messing about like that if she's really ill. We'd better take her to Casualty.
Nick I had to go there once. They kept me waiting for hours before they saw me.

Liz They won't keep us waiting. Not when they know that it's a baby who is ill. Shall we go?
Mike Yes. Right. My car's parked outside.
Chrissie Somebody come with me.
Carol I will.
Liz And me.
Mike Come on, then.

(**Mike** *and the three girls prepare to go out with* **Chrissie** *carrying the baby*)

Phil What if Hazel comes back? What do we tell her?
Liz We'll ring you from the hospital as soon as we know something. Come on. Let's not hang about.

(**Mike**, **Carol**, **Liz** *and* **Chrissie** *go out*)

Nev What do we do now? Anyone fancy a beer?
Phil No, thanks.
Nick No.
Nev Bit of music?
Nick No. Give it a rest, Nev.
Phil That baby worries me. Hazel's going to be pretty upset when she hears about this.
Nick I wonder where she is. She should have been back before this, shouldn't she?
Nev Probably some hold-up at the interview. She wouldn't know how many were queuing up for the job. The manager might have been late in starting. Anything like that.
Phil I suppose so.

```
┌─────── Characters for Scene Five ───────┐
│           Phil      Nick                │
│           Nev       Carol               │
│           Nick      Chrissie            │
│           Hazel     Liz                 │
└─────────────────────────────────────────┘
```

Scene Five In the Living Room about half an hour later. **Phil**, **Nev** and **Nick** are handing round cups of coffee. The party is coming to an end.

Nick Good coffee. Thanks Nev.
Phil It's daft really. We should know where Hazel is.
Nev We were too busy arguing about where we should have the party.
Nick Some party. I should be getting off home. I've got an early start tomorrow.
Phil You get off then, Nick. I'll stay here until Hazel gets back.
Nick No. I'll hang on until we hear from the hospital.

(**Hazel** comes in)

Phil Where have you been? We were worried.
Hazel What sort of a welcome is that? You ought to be congratulating me. I got the job.
Phil That's great.
Hazel Yes. They took two of us on. The manager was late getting there and then he asked us two for a drink after. I didn't want to refuse, seeing he'd just taken me on.
Nev Oh.
Hazel But where is everybody? Gone home? What happened to the party? Where's

	Chrissie? Was Nicola good? (*She moves towards the bedroom door*)
Phil	Don't go in the bedroom, Hazel. Nicola's not here.
Hazel	What?
Nev	She didn't seem well. We thought the best thing would be to have a doctor look at her.
Hazel	A doctor? Where is she?
Phil	We didn't know who her doctor was so they've taken her to hospital.
Hazel	To hospital? Where? What's the matter with her? Oh, my God. Where is she?
Phil	It's all right, Hazel. Calm down. I don't think it's serious.
Hazel	Not serious? How do you know? You must have thought it was serious to send her to hospital. Is it the General? Tell me where she is! I've got to go to her.
Nev	It probably is the General. But there's no point in going there yet.
Hazel	What do you mean 'probably'? Don't you know?
Phil	Take it easy, Hazel. They're going to ring as soon as they know anything. We just have to wait.
Hazel	Wait! (*Goes to door*) I'm not waiting. Poor little thing! I should never have gone to that interview. I must have been out of my mind leaving her with you lot.
Phil	Hazel! Listen!
Hazel	No. I'll have to wait hours for a bus at this time of night. I'd better try for a taxi. (*Goes to phone*)
Phil	Don't use that. They may be ringing through any minute.
Hazel	Oh, shut up.

(*The phone rings. Before* **Hazel** *can get to it,* **Phil** *picks it up*)

Phil Yes, it's me ... Yes ... Yes. Oh, that's great. Hazel was very worried. Yes ... Okay ... Fine ... Yes, that's good ... About ten minutes? ... Right. We'll be here. (*He puts the phone down*) Nicola's fine and they're on their way home.

(*10 minutes passes, during which time* **Hazel**, **Nick**, **Phil** *and* **Nev** *sit in silence. Then* **Chrissie** *and* **Carol** *arrive back.* **Chrissie** *is carrying the baby.* **Hazel** *rushes to take it from her*)

Hazel Nicola!
Phil Did they keep you waiting long?
Carol No. They were very good.
Chrissie What took up the time was the examination.
Liz They were very thorough.
Chrissie We were relieved when they found nothing wrong.
Carol One of the doctors said it could have been teething.
Hazel She's peacefully asleep now, anyway. I'll put her down.

(**Hazel** *takes the baby into the bedroom*)

Carol They gave her something at the hospital.
Nick All's well that end's well. I'll be off.
Nev Me too.
Carol Yes. She'll want to be rid of us now things are all right again.

(**Hazel** *comes back*)

Phil Is she all right?
Hazel Yes, of course she's all right. What on

74

	earth did you want to go dragging her off to hospital for? Must have frightened the life out of her – a strange place like that.
Chrissie	It seemed the best thing to do at the time.
Hazel	Did it? I should never have agreed to having a party here in the first place. No wonder Nicola got upset.
Phil	Now, just a minute, Hazel...
Hazel	I blame you for this, Phil. I thought you'd take charge of things here. I shan't forgive you in a hurry.

⟨5⟩

Work on the play

⟨1⟩ Develop the Plot

Chrissie isn't giving Nev much support in his efforts to make sure she goes to the party. Hazel probably has a point about the noise. However, it is finally agreed that the party will be held in her flat. Does Nev agree to do something about keeping the noise down? Does he persuade Chrissie to come in on his side? Or does Hazel feel that she is being a bit mean, since babysitting is so important to her? What part does Hazel's boyfriend Phil play in the argument over where to have the party? Discuss the line each character might take and then act it out.

⟨2⟩ Develop the Plot

If someone invited to the party, like Frankie, brings along an unknown or unwelcome guest is that all right? If someone invited brings along two or three unknown mates, is that all right, too? If two or three totally uninvited gatecrashers come along and try to get in, what happens? Discuss what the three characters might decide to do and then act out their conversation.

③ **Develop the Plot**

Cliff and Wayne are not allowed in and they go away without violence or fighting. Does Lee plead for them or does he turn nasty and threaten violence? Are Cliff and Wayne aggressive, too, or do they go quietly, not liking the look of the party? Does Lee go with them? Does Frankie go with him or is she getting fed up with him? If violence is threatened, are Phil and Nev and Nick big enough to put Cliff and Wayne (and Lee if he throws his weight about, too) off that idea? Discuss how the characters might react in this situation and then act out the rest of the scene until Cliff and Wayne (and, perhaps, Lee and Frankie) have gone.

④ **Develop the Plot**

An extra scene: at the hospital. How are Chrissie, Liz and Carol received at Casualty? How do they explain what seems to be wrong with the baby? Are the nurses sympathetic? Do they ask where Nicola's mother is? Do they ask who her usual doctor is? What happens when the girls cannot tell them this? Is the doctor helpful or not? What does he or she tell them about the baby to reassure them that she is quite all right? Does the doctor praise them for bringing the baby to hospital anyway, rather than run any risks?

⑤ **Finish the Play**

Is Hazel being unreasonable and ungrateful or was taking the baby to hospital rather a panic move? Who was really responsible for the decision to take her? Would Chrissie have been better off looking after the baby on her own? Discuss the sort of things that might be said by Phil and Nev to calm Hazel down and then act out the final scene.

Projects and Assignments

Who are the Beasts?

1a Casting
You are going to present the second scene on television. Describe the people you would pick to play *three* of the characters.

1b Background
If this play were on television you might need to show a few shots of the hunt. Describe what you would see if either you showed a few of the huntsmen and women, or you showed a long shot of the hunt in pursuit of the fox.

2a The Set
Describe the set you would use for the scene in the Research Station. You will need to think of the caged animals and the kind of equipment used such as, perhaps, an operating table. Where would the materials for the experiments be stored? In cupboards or on shelves? You can decide whether the scene will be for a stage or television performance and you can draw and label a ground plan of the set you are going to use.

Situation Vacant

1a The Set
It is suggested that this play is done on a bare stage with only furniture and props. List the things you would put on stage to suggest an office. Note that Miss Starr has a computer.

1b Sound Effects
The follow-up work suggests places where sound effects could be used in this play (see ②, ⑤ and ⑥, Develop the Plot, pages 26 to 27, and ⑦ Finish the Play, page 27). However there is no firm indication of what the sounds might be. Go through the play, and

decide on suitable sound effects, making a note of precisely where each comes in the play.

2a **Lighting Effects**
Dimming the lights or making them brighter or altering the colour of the lighting can create menacing or reassuring effects on stage. Make a plan showing where you would change the lighting through the play, saying why you would change it, and indicating the lighting changes you would make.

2b **Playing a Role**
Pick one of the characters, read through the part and then describe how you would dress and how you think the character might react and feel as the lines are spoken and how you, as actor, would show these reactions and feelings.

The Concert

1 **Casting**
The Manager and Barbara Wade have two small parts in the last scene. Describe the sort of person you would pick to play each part.

2a **Stage Directions**
If, in the first scene, all the characters are simply sitting down, the result will be rather static or fixed and perhaps dull. Suggest some things that the characters might do to bring movement into this scene to enliven it. For instance, if Mrs Watson simply brings in a tray of tea or Mr Watson fiddles with the television, that could break up the static scene. Try, however, to think of other things they might do.

2b **Direction**
There is a bit of feeling between the members of the group in Scene Two. How would you show this by telling the actors to move and behave? For instance when, in the fourth line, Adam says 'You're asking us?' (page 31) is he surprised? Does he pause before he says it? Is Colin, in the next line, annoyed with Dave? If so, does he speak sharply? Work through the scene,

as if you were a director, down to the line 'Dave: You want to swap me for Ben Ramsay?' writing down how you would tell the actors to say their lines and what they might do.

Boat Trip

1a Sound Effects
You are producing this as a radio play. List the sound effects you would need in the first scene. Apart from the music and the taped radio voice, think of the sea and the sound of rowing.

1b Casting
Describe the kind of people you would pick to play the parts of Lena, Alec and Brant.

2a Narration
You are going to present Scene Five (page 47) as part of a promotion programme for the play. Write, either as narrator or presenter, the introduction to this scene to tell the audience or listeners what has gone before.

2b Direction
In Scene Five, the crooks are uneasy. Write down the sort of directions you might give if you were director to the actors in this scene, from where Alec says 'Well?' (page 49) to Lena's line, 'It's dangerous to go up there . . .' (page 50) telling them how to behave and how to say their lines.

2c A Review
You know the play. Write, as if you were a theatre critic, your review of it.

Let's have a Party

1a Casting
Pick three characters from the play and describe the kind of person you would choose to play each one. You will need to say about how old the character should be and describe the way in which you think he or she would be dressed.

1b **The Set**
If you were putting on the play, you would need to think about the room in the flat where the scene is set. List some of the things you would need to have on stage, such as a phone and possibly a carrycot or something like that for this first scene. What sort of furniture would you need?

2 **Soliloquy**
In some plays a person alone on a stage will say his or her thoughts aloud. This is called a 'soliloquy'. Hazel, in this play, is a single parent with a small child. Is she sorry her husband has left her? Is she relieved? Is she worried about how she will manage in the future with the baby? As if you were the character, write her thoughts when she is alone before the play begins as she talks to herself or soliloquises about her life.

General Questions

1a **Publicity Artwork**
Design a poster for one of these plays.

1b **Publicity Copy**
Write a short piece of publicity material for one of these plays for a newspaper column. You will need to give a title and a very short description of what the play is about.

2a **Presentation**
Which of these plays would be more effective – or more suitable for – production on a stage or on the radio or on film or video tape? Deal with each play in turn, suggesting a suitable form in which to present it giving your reasons.